THE BUSINESS OF FOOD

The Strategies for Success in the Restaurant and Hospitality Industry

By Chiemela Solace

CHIEMELA SOLACE

THE STRATEGIES FOR SUCCESS IN THE RESTAURANT AND HOSPITALITY INDUSTRY

All rights reserved. No part of this [publication/work/material] may be reproduced, distributed, or transmitted in any form or by any means, including photocopying, recording, or other electronic or mechanical methods, without the prior written permission of the copyright holder, except in the case of brief quotations embodied in critical reviews and certain other noncommercial uses permitted by copyright law.

Copyright © (2023) [Chiemela Solace].

Table of Contents

CHAPTER ONE: 7
INTRODUCTION TO THE RESTAURANT AND
HOSPITALITY INDUSTRY 7

CHAPTER TWO: 11
MARKET RESEARCH AND TARGET AUDIENCE ANALYSIS
.... 11

CHAPTER THREE: 16
MENU DEVELOPMENT AND PRICING STRATEGIES 16

CHAPTER FOUR: 20
MARKETING AND PROMOTIONAL STRATEGIES FOR
RESTAURANTS AND HOTELS 20

CHAPTER FIVE: 26
RESTAURANT AND HOTEL OPERATIONS MANAGEMENT
.... 26

CHAPTER SIX: 29
STAFF TRAINING AND DEVELOPMENT 29

CHAPTER SEVEN: 32

THE STRATEGIES FOR SUCCESS IN THE RESTAURANT AND HOSPITALITY INDUSTRY

Customer Service and Hospitality Best Practices 32

CHAPTER EIGHT: **36**
Financial Management and Profit Maximization 36

CHAPTER NINE: **40**
Legal and Regulatory Issues in the Restaurant and Hospitality Industry 40

CHAPTER TEN: **43**
Trends and Innovations in the Restaurant and Hospitality Industry 43

Tips on how to stay updated to trends in the restaurant and hospitality industry *44*

Conclusion 47

CHIEMELA SOLACE

THE STRATEGIES FOR SUCCESS IN THE RESTAURANT AND HOSPITALITY INDUSTRY

Chapter One:

Introduction to the Restaurant and Hospitality Industry

The restaurant and hospitality industry is a dynamic and diverse sector that plays a vital role in the global economy. From fine dining establishments to fast food chains, and hotels to bed and breakfasts, the industry caters to a wide range of customer preferences and budgets. With the rise of food culture and the increasing importance of travel and tourism, the demand for high-quality food and accommodation continues to grow.

However, the restaurant and hospitality industry is also highly competitive, with a high rate of failure among new businesses. To succeed in this industry, it is crucial for entrepreneurs and managers to have a solid understanding of the key factors that drive success. This includes market research and target audience analysis, menu development and pricing strategies, marketing, and promotional tactics, effective operations management, and financial planning.

The restaurant and hospitality industry is a vast and complex sector that encompasses a wide range of businesses, from independent cafes to multinational hotel chains. It is an industry that is both deeply personal and highly commercial, relying on the creation of memorable experiences and the satisfaction of customers' needs and desires.

Success in the restaurant and hospitality industry requires a combination of creativity, business acumen, and attention to detail. It is an industry that is constantly evolving, with new trends and technologies emerging all the time. To succeed, business owners and managers must be adaptable and open to change, while also staying true to their vision and values.

THE STRATEGIES FOR SUCCESS IN THE RESTAURANT AND HOSPITALITY INDUSTRY

In this book, we will explore the various aspects of the business food, with a focus on strategies for success in the restaurant and hospitality industry, we will also cover topics such as market research and target audience analysis, menu development, and pricing strategies, marketing, and promotional tactics, effective operations management, and financial planning. We will also delve into the latest trends and innovations in the industry, and discuss best practices in customer service and staff development.

Whether you are an aspiring entrepreneur, a seasoned professional, or simply a food and hospitality enthusiast, we hope that this publication will provide you with valuable insights and practical knowledge that you can apply to your own business or career.

CHIEMELA SOLACE

Chapter Two:

Market Research and Target Audience Analysis

As a business starter, one of the most important things you can do to increase your chances of success is to conduct thorough market research and identify your target audience. This involves gathering and analyzing data on your customers, competitors, and industry to inform your decision-making and marketing efforts.

Market research is the process of gathering and analyzing data about your market, customers, and competition to inform your business decisions. It can be conducted through a variety of methods, including surveys, focus groups, interviews, and online research. Market research allows you to better understand your target audience and their needs, preferences, and behaviors, as well as the competitive landscape in which you operate.

Target audience analysis is the process of identifying and understanding the characteristics, needs, and behaviors of the customers you are most likely to sell to. This includes identifying your target demographics, such as age, gender, income, education level, and geographic location. It also involves understanding the needs and preferences of your target audience, as well as their decision-making processes and behaviors.

By conducting market research and target audience analysis, you can gain valuable insights that will help you:

- Develop a clear marketing message and positioning that resonates with your target audience

- Create a product or service that meets the needs and preferences of your target audience

- Set pricing that is competitive and attractive to your target audience

THE STRATEGIES FOR SUCCESS IN THE RESTAURANT AND HOSPITALITY INDUSTRY

- Identify the most effective marketing channels and tactics for reaching your target audience

- Make informed business decisions based on data-driven insights

The following are the successful ways for conducting market research and get a targeted audience for your business:

- Start by identifying your business goals and the questions you want to answer through your market research. This will help you focus your efforts and ensure that you are gathering the most relevant and useful data.

- Use a combination of primary and secondary research methods to gather a well-rounded view of your market and customers. Primary research methods, such as surveys and focus groups, allow you to gather original data directly from your target audience. Secondary research methods, such as online searches and industry reports, provide background information and context.

- Analyze and interpret your research data carefully, using statistical analysis software or other tools as needed. Look for patterns and trends, and pay attention to both positive and negative feedback.

- Keep your target audience front and center as you conduct your research and analysis. Use customer personas or other tools to help you understand and empathize with your target customers.

- Don't be afraid to ask for help or advice from more experienced professionals. Market research and target audience analysis can be complex and time-consuming, and getting guidance from someone with expertise in your industry can save you time and effort.

THE STRATEGIES FOR SUCCESS IN THE RESTAURANT AND HOSPITALITY INDUSTRY

Following these ways in conducting market research and target audience analysis, you can give your business the best and set yourself up for long-term success.

Chapter Three:

Menu Development and Pricing Strategies

One of the important decisions you will need to make is what to include on your menu and how to price your items. The menu and pricing strategy you choose can have a big impact on your overall business success, as they can affect everything from customer satisfaction to profitability.

Menu development is the process of creating a list of items that your business will offer to customers. This includes deciding what types of food and drink to serve, as well as how to present and organize your menu. When developing your menu, it's important to consider factors such as your target audience, your competition, your business goals, and your operational capabilities.

Pricing strategy is the process of determining the price at which you will sell your products or services. There are many different pricing strategies that

THE STRATEGIES FOR SUCCESS IN THE RESTAURANT AND HOSPITALITY INDUSTRY

businesses can use, and the right strategy will depend on your business goals and the market you operate in. Some common pricing strategies include cost-based pricing, value-based pricing, and competition-based pricing.

Here are some useful steps for developing an effective menu and pricing strategy for a business:

- Start by identifying your target audience and the types of food and drink that will appeal to them. Consider factors such as demographics, preferences, and budget.

- Research your competition to see what types of items and prices they offer. Use this information to differentiate your menu and find your own niche in the market.

- Determine your operational capabilities, including your kitchen and serving staff, equipment, and supply chain. This will help you decide what types of items you can realistically prepare and serve.

- Consider your business goals when developing your menu and pricing strategy. Do you want to focus on high-end, gourmet items with higher prices, or do you want to offer more affordable casual options?

- Use cost-based pricing to determine the minimum price at which you can sell your items and still turn a profit. Take into account the cost of ingredients, labor, and overhead.

- Experiment with different pricing strategies to see what works best for your business. Don't be afraid to make changes based on customer feedback and market conditions.

- Use menu engineering techniques to optimize your menu for profitability. This can include rearranging items, using visual cues, and highlighting high-profit items.

THE STRATEGIES FOR SUCCESS IN THE RESTAURANT AND HOSPITALITY INDUSTRY

- Consider offering promotions and discounts to drive sales and attract new customers.

Chapter Four:

Marketing and Promotional Strategies for Restaurants and Hotels

In the marketing and promotion of restaurants and hotels, it is important to have a strong marketing and promotional strategy in place to attract and retain customers. Marketing is the process of promoting and selling your products or services, while promotion refers to the specific tactics and activities you use to reach and persuade your target audience.

There are many different marketing and promotional strategies that restaurants and hotels can use, and the right strategy will depend on your business goals, target audience, and budget. Some common strategies include:

- **Traditional advertising:** Using print, radio, or television ads to reach a wide audience.

THE STRATEGIES FOR SUCCESS IN THE RESTAURANT AND HOSPITALITY INDUSTRY

- **Digital marketing:** Using online channels such as social media, email, and website advertising to reach and engage customers.

- **Content marketing:** Creating and distributing valuable, relevant, and consistent content to attract and retain a clearly defined audience.

- **Public relations**: Building relationships with media outlets and other influencers to get your business featured in news articles and other content.

- **Word-of-mouth marketing:** Encouraging customers to share their experiences with your business with their friends and social networks.

- **Loyalty programs:** Offering rewards and incentives to repeat customers to encourage loyalty and repeat business.

From previous experience, some effective marketing and promotional strategies for your restaurant or hotel business can be deduced as follows:

- Start by identifying your target audience and your unique selling points. What makes your business different from your competition, and what will appeal to your target customers?

- Develop a clear marketing message and branding that reflects your business values and personality.

- Research your competition to see what marketing and promotional strategies they are using and consider how you can differentiate your business.

- Set marketing and sales goals and create a budget to support your efforts.

- Use a mix of traditional and digital marketing channels to reach a wide audience. Consider the specific needs and preferences of your target audience when choosing your channels.

- Use data and analytics to track the effectiveness of your marketing and promotional efforts. This will help you make informed decisions about where to allocate.

Here are some additional tips for developing an effective marketing and promotional strategy for your restaurant or hotel business:

- Use content marketing to showcase your business and engage with potential customers. This can include creating a blog, posting on social media, or creating videos or other multimedia content.

- Leverage public relations to get your business featured in the media. This can include writing press releases, pitching story ideas to journalists, and developing relationships with influencers.

- Encourage word-of-mouth marketing by providing excellent customer service and encouraging customers to share their experiences with your business on social media and review sites.

- Consider implementing a loyalty program to reward repeat customers and encourage loyalty. This can include offering discounts, freebies, or other perks to customers who frequently visit your business.

- Use promotional tactics to drive sales and attract new customers. This can include offering discounts, running contests or giveaways, or hosting special events or promotions.

- Be consistent in your marketing and promotional efforts, and stay true to your brand and values. This will help you build trust and credibility with your target audience.

THE STRATEGIES FOR SUCCESS IN THE RESTAURANT AND HOSPITALITY INDUSTRY

You can effectively reach and engage your target customers, drive sales and revenue, and build a successful business in the restaurant and hospitality industry using the above mentioned tips.

Chapter Five:

Restaurant and Hotel Operations Management

As a business starter in the restaurant and hospitality industry, effective operations management is crucial to your success. Operations management refers to the planning, organizing, and controlling of the resources and processes that your business uses to produce and deliver products and services. This includes everything from food and beverage preparation to customer service, from financial management to staffing.

Here are some key areas of operations management that are particularly important for restaurants and hotels:

- **Menu planning:** Develop a menu that meets the needs and preferences of your target audience, while also considering factors such as cost, operational feasibility, and food trends.

THE STRATEGIES FOR SUCCESS IN THE RESTAURANT AND HOSPITALITY INDUSTRY

- **Kitchen and bar management**: Ensuring that food and drink are prepared and served to a high standard, with a focus on quality, safety, and efficiency.

- **Customer service:** Providing excellent customer service to create a positive customer experience and encourage repeat business.

- **Financial management:** Managing the financial aspects of your business, including budgeting, forecasting, and cost control.

- **Staff management:** Hiring, training, and managing a team of employees to deliver top-quality service and support your business goals.

Here are some tips for effective managing the operations of your restaurant or hotel as a business starter:

- Start by developing a clear vision and mission for your business, and use this to guide your operations management decisions.

- Create a detailed business plan that outlines your operational processes and procedures, to ascertain business goals.

Chapter Six:

Staff Training and Development

Investing in the training and development of your staff can have a big impact on the success of your business. Staff training and development refers to the process of providing employees with the knowledge, skills, and abilities they need to perform their jobs effectively and achieve their potential. This can include both formal and informal training, as well as ongoing development opportunities.

Here are some key benefits of investing in staff training and development:

- **Improved performance:** By providing your staff with the skills and knowledge they need to do their jobs effectively, you can increase productivity and efficiency.

- **Increased customer satisfaction:** Well-trained staff are better equipped to deliver high-quality service, which can lead to increased customer satisfaction and loyalty.

- **Enhanced employee engagement:** By investing in your staff, you show them that you value their contributions and are committed to their development. This can lead to increased employee engagement and retention.

- **Improved business reputation:** A well-trained and knowledgeable staff can enhance your business's reputation and credibility.

Here are some tips for implementing an effective staff training and development program in a business:

- Start by identifying the specific training and development needs of your staff. This can include assessing their current skills and knowledge, as well as their career goals and aspirations.

THE STRATEGIES FOR SUCCESS IN THE RESTAURANT AND HOSPITALITY INDUSTRY

- Develop a clear training and development plan that outlines your goals and objectives.

Chapter Seven:

Customer Service and Hospitality Best Practices

Providing excellent customer service is crucial to your success. Customer service refers to the interactions and support that you provide to your customers, from the moment they first make contact with your business until long after they have left. Hospitality best practices are the industry standards and guidelines that help businesses deliver high-quality service and create a positive customer experience.

Here are some key benefits of providing excellent customer service and following hospitality best practices:

- **Increased customer satisfaction:** By providing timely, helpful, and friendly service, you can increase customer satisfaction and loyalty.

THE STRATEGIES FOR SUCCESS IN THE RESTAURANT AND HOSPITALITY INDUSTRY

- **Improved business reputation:** A reputation for excellent customer service can attract new customers and enhance your business's credibility.

- **Increased revenue:** Happy customers are more likely to return and recommend your business to others, which can lead to increased sales and revenue.

Here are some tips for providing excellent customer service and following hospitality best practices as a business starter:

- Start by setting clear customer service standards and expectations for your staff. This can include guidelines on things like greetings, response times, and problem-solving.

- Train your staff on customer service and hospitality best practices, and provide ongoing development opportunities to keep their skills and knowledge up to date.

- Encourage a culture of customer service excellence within your business. This can include recognizing and rewarding staff for their customer service efforts and soliciting feedback from customers.

- Use customer feedback and data to continuously improve your customer service and hospitality practices. This can include tracking customer satisfaction scores and analyzing customer complaints and compliments.

- Take a proactive approach to customer service by anticipating and addressing customer needs and concerns before they become problems.

- Foster a friendly and welcoming atmosphere in your business, and make an effort to personalize the customer experience whenever possible.

THE STRATEGIES FOR SUCCESS IN THE RESTAURANT AND HOSPITALITY INDUSTRY

Using the following tips provided above, you can create a positive and memorable customer experience that sets your business apart from the competition.

Chapter Eight:

Financial Management and Profit Maximization

The reason for every business is to gain profit, most business owners don't know how to maximize their profit which leads to the failure of many businesses. Effective financial management and profit maximization are crucial to your success. Financial management refers to the process of managing the financial resources of your business, including budgeting, forecasting, and cost control. Profit maximization refers to the process of maximizing the profitability of your business by increasing revenues and minimizing costs.

Here are some key areas of financial management and profit maximization that are particularly important for business starters:

THE STRATEGIES FOR SUCCESS IN THE RESTAURANT AND HOSPITALITY INDUSTRY

- **Budgeting:** Creating a detailed plan that outlines your expected income and expenses, and allocating resources accordingly.

- **Forecasting:** Predicting future financial performance based on past data and industry trends, and using this information to inform your decision-making.

- **Cost control:** Monitoring and managing expenses to ensure that they are in line with your budget and business goals.

- **Pricing strategy:** Determining the price at which you will sell your products or services, taking into account your costs, competition, and target audience.

- **Revenue generation:** Identifying and pursuing opportunities to increase revenue, such as expanding your product or service offerings, increasing prices, or attracting new customers.

Here are some tips for effective managing of your finances and maximizing profitability in business:

- Start by creating a detailed business plan that includes financial projections and a budget. This will help you set clear financial goals and track your progress.

- Use financial tools and software to manage your finances and analyze your data. This can include accounting software, budgeting tools, and financial modeling software.

- Monitor your financial performance regularly, and use data and analytics to inform your decision-making.

- Focus on cost control by identifying and addressing unnecessary or inefficient expenses.

THE STRATEGIES FOR SUCCESS IN THE RESTAURANT AND HOSPITALITY INDUSTRY

Chapter Nine:

Legal and Regulatory Issues in the Restaurant and Hospitality Industry

In the restaurant and hospitality industry, it is important to be aware of the various legal and regulatory issues that can affect your business. These can include issues related to food safety, employment law, contracts, and licenses and permits.

Here are some key legal and regulatory issues that you should be aware of as a business starter:

- **Food safety:** Restaurants and hotels are subject to strict food safety regulations to prevent the spread of foodborne illnesses. This can include requirements related to food storage, preparation, and handling.

- **Employment law:** There are various laws and regulations related to the employment of staff, including minimum wage, overtime, and discrimination. It is important to familiarize yourself with these laws and ensure that you are in compliance.

- **Contracts:** When entering into agreements with suppliers, contractors, or other partners, it is important to have a clear and legally binding contract in place to protect your interests.

- **Licenses and permits:** Depending on your location and business type, you may be required to obtain various licenses and permits to operate legally. This can include things like liquor licenses, food handling permits, and business licenses.

Here are some tips for navigating legal and regulatory issues as a business starter:

- Start by researching the specific laws and regulations that apply to your business. This can include consulting with an attorney or checking with your local government or industry association.

- Implement policies and procedures to ensure compliance with food safety regulations and employment laws.

- Use contracts to clearly define the terms of your agreements with suppliers, contractors, and other partners.

- Obtain any necessary licenses and permits before starting your business.

- Stay up to date with changes to laws and regulations that may affect your business.

By following these tips and staying informed about legal and regulatory issues, you can protect your business and ensure that you are operating in compliance with the law.

Chapter Ten:

Trends and Innovations in the Restaurant and Hospitality Industry

The restaurant and hospitality industry is constantly evolving and adapting to new trends and innovations. As a business owner, it's important to stay up-to-date with these changes in order to stay competitive and attract customers.

Here are some key trends and innovations in the restaurant and hospitality industry that you should be aware of as a business owner:

- **Plant-based menu options:** There has been an increasing demand for plant-based menu options, such as vegetarian and vegan dishes, as more people adopt plant-based diets.

- **Technology integration:** Many restaurants and hotels are integrating technology into their operations, such as using online ordering systems, mobile payments, and customer loyalty apps.

- **Sustainability:** Many customers are looking for businesses that prioritize sustainability, such as by using eco-friendly materials or sourcing ingredients locally.

- **Customer experience:** Enhancing the customer experience is becoming increasingly important in the restaurant and hospitality industry. This can include things like personalized recommendations, immersive dining experiences, and interactive elements.

Tips on how to stay updated to trends in the restaurant and hospitality industry

Here are some tips for staying up to date with trends and innovations in the restaurant and hospitality industry as a business owner:

THE STRATEGIES FOR SUCCESS IN THE RESTAURANT AND HOSPITALITY INDUSTRY

- Stay informed about industry trends and innovations by reading industry news and attending industry events and conferences.

- Consider conducting market research to gather insights about your customers' preferences and expectations.

- Be open to trying new things and experimenting with your menu or operations.

- Look for opportunities to differentiate your business by offering unique or innovative products or services.

- Consider working with a business coach or mentor who can provide guidance and support as you navigate the industry.

By staying up to date with trends and innovations and being open to trying new things, you can stay competitive and attract customers in the dynamic restaurant and hospitality industry.

CHIEMELA SOLACE

Conclusion

There are a number of strategies that can help businesses in the restaurant and hospitality industry succeed. These include offering a unique and high-quality product or service, understanding and targeting your audience, creating a strong brand and marketing strategy, managing finances effectively, and building a strong team. In order to stand out in a crowded and competitive market, it is essential for businesses in this industry to focus on these key areas and continually strive to improve and adapt.

www.ingramcontent.com/pod-product-compliance
Lightning Source LLC
Chambersburg PA
CBHW050316220526
45465CB00005B/2023